PEACE
THE ENEMY OF
FREEDOM

Publisher's Cataloging in Publication
(Prepared by Quality Books Inc.)

Webster-Doyle, Terrence, 1940-
    Peace, the enemy of freedom : the myth of nonviolence /
Terrence Webster-Doyle. —
    p. cm. — (Sane and intelligent living series)
    ISBN 0-942941-12-8

    1. Peace.   2. Causes of war.   3. Interpersonal conflict.
    4. Social conflict.   I. Title.   II. Series

    JX1953   327.1'72

Library of Congress Catalog Number: 90-85198

PEACE — THE ENEMY OF FREEDOM
The Myth of Nonviolence
by
Terrence Webster-Doyle

Design & Production, Editor:
Charlene Koonce

Cover Design:
Robert Howard

Advisor:
John Shoolery

Typesetting:
I'm Your Type

Creative Consultant:
Jean Webster-Doyle

Published by:
Atrium Society
Post Office Box 816
Middlebury, Vermont 05753
Tel: (802) 388-0922
Fax: (802) 388-1027
For book order information:
(800) 848-6021

Table of Contents

Peace, **The Enemy of Freedom** — *The Myth of Nonviolence* is the fourth in a series of books on psychological conditioning entitled **The Sane and Intelligent Living Series.** The first book of the series, **Growing Up Sane** — *Understanding the Conditioned Mind,* focuses on the destructive nature of psychological conditioning by examining its influence on our social structures and its root within the psyche itself. The second book in the series, **Brave New Child**, examines a solution to the problem of psychological conditioning. The third and fourth books in the series are: **The Religious Impulse** — *A Quest for Innocence,* which contrasts contradictory religious practices with the religious mind, free of conditioning; and **Peace, The Enemy of Freedom** — *The Myth of Nonviolence,* an enquiry into the paradoxical nature of creating peace.

Forthcoming books include: **Atrium** — *The Foundation of Learning;* **Student to Student** — *Conversations on War and Peace;* **Teacher to Teacher** — *Conversations on Education and Freedom;* and **The Child in Changing Times** — *A Curriculum on Psychological Conditioning.*

Each book, although part of a series, is complete in itself. The focus of all the books is to examine the nature and structure of conflict — inwardly and outwardly. Each book offers a different perspective on this theme.

Author's Note

In this book, Peace — the Enemy of Freedom, I will not be approaching the issue of peace, or any issue of human behavior, in the conventional manner. I am not writing an intellectual dissertation on the subject of peace. I am not a scholar, nor am I advocating a study of peace. I am not suggesting that I am an expert in the field of human relations; I am only a human being who is serious about these issues. I am not advocating any political response to this issue of peace, nor am I encouraging any religious perspective. I am not asking anyone to believe in a particular philosophical ideology, and I am not interested in economic revolutions. Nor am I concerned with creating Utopian communities in which to live. In essence, I am not promoting any "way." As I see it, all ways are contrivances, avoidances of the *fact* of who we are and what we are *actually* doing. I am attempting to look simply, without any judgment, comparison, or evaluation, at what is true and what is false — to see the actual, the real, the thing itself. This may sound either too radical or too simplistic. It is neither: It is the only thing we can "do" — and by this I do not mean the traditional "doing" that we are used to. We have been conditioned to think that we can "do" something to bring about peace and to end war. I am seriously questioning this assumption. I am proposing — with utmost urgency — that what we think of as creative and noble action aimed at bringing about a change in behavior, as in the case of war and peace, is *destructive.* I am not asserting this; it is not a conclusion. It is simply the subject of our observation.

What this book asks is simple yet difficult: that we suspend our beliefs, opinions, and educated knowledge to look anew. We cannot approach understanding what it means to live in peace, in the absence of war, through the past. The roots of conflict can only be approached in the present, as it occurs. The conflict that we call war, the militarized aggression that kills human beings, is rooted in us, in our brains, in the way we think, feel and act. Internal conflict is projected outward and creates global conflict. The world is created by us; we are responsible for devastation and a vicious, competitive, divisive way of life. Assigning the state of the world to any outside force is a mistake.

As the author of this book, I feel an urgent concern for us to address the issue of war and peace directly in ourselves. Some people have said that my "appeal" is too emotional and not intellectual enough. One must feel! Feeling, not emotionalism or sentiment, is the outcome of direct contact with life.

This is not an intellectual book. This book offers observations on the nature and structure of human behavior and how we create and sustain conflict through our usual habitual conditioned approaches to life. My hope is that the reader will be challenged to question what is being said, not to accept or reject what the author is sharing, no matter how assertive or opinionated it may seem. I feel that we need to stop and seriously reflect on our conventional solutions to the problems of life, to see if we are, paradoxically, creating further conflict in the name of peace.

INTRODUCTION

The intent of this book is to bring about an understanding of conflict: it is not an attempt to create peace. This understanding is not arrived at through an intellectual comparison of ideas on the subject, no matter how noble, eloquent, or inspirational the ideas might be. Understanding intellectually involves time: "Peace will come in the future if we just..." The intent of this book is to stimulate or awaken insight into what prevents peace — not in the future, but now.

Peace cannot come through time, through a process of analysis. The cause of conflict, that which prevents peace, exists in us each moment and is acted out only in the moment — now. Understanding uncovers the movement of conflict as it reveals itself in our daily lives. War is the outward manifestation of the inward disorder and discord of the divided, fragmented human being. Life, as it is lived now, is a battlefield — a competitive "cutthroat," aggressive process of self-attainment. Conflict must be looked at in our day-to-day living. We are at war in ourselves, in our relationships. Peace is only an ideal, that which we wish for. This is a fact.

Observations into the nature and structure of conflict are offered mainly as "working hypotheses" for the reader to use to look for him or herself, to see if these are true or accurate reflections of what actually creates disorder, war.

The observations or vignettes which follow are

presented one to a page so that the reader has the opportunity to reflect or ponder on what is being said. In traditional literature on human behavior, the reader is presented with a thesis and then must read on through pages of substantiation intended to prove the validity of the thesis. Here, observations or insights are offered mainly as questions, so that the reader might engage in a process of directly finding out for him or herself if what is being said is true — or not.

A question holds the intellectual mind in abeyance. If an immediate answer were given, that would cut off the process of enquiry. A question, if held, will lead to observation. Observation, or enquiry, is that faculty of mind that looks anew at life, without the intervention of what one already knows, which is the past. What is needed in understanding that which creates conflict is not more information on conflict, but rather insight into its immediate cause. As one questions, there is an immediate temporary cessation of conditioned reactive thinking and beliefs. It is this cessation of reaction — when conditioning is in abeyance — that frees the brain from its habitual, divisive compulsion for violence. The question breaks the pattern that drives the brain in its relentless fixations.

As one questions, as one observes what that questioning reveals to the mind, to awareness, one has the opportunity to be free of conditioned thinking and action. This allows a space for intelligence to enter, so that there can be profound insight into one's own behavior. So questioning, observation, is *vitally* important in understanding what causes war and prevents peace! Once one is questioning, enquiring without concluding, the process takes on a life of its own. One doesn't need to read more about it, one simply observes, directly, one's own conditioned state of mind — the conditioning that creates and sustains conflict individually and globally. Then one can put down this book, at any point, and look for oneself. All this book can do is to stimulate one's observation and point to what creates conflict, not intellectually but actually. In this moment of observation, there is immediate insight into the causes of war, at the source.

Therefore, this book is written in such a way as to enhance this faculty of observation and insight, so that as one reads, one will not accumulate more knowledge but will, rather, begin to actually observe — come into direct contact with — conflict as it is, and, in so doing, learn about its origins. This learning is not the storing of facts in memory, as one would do when studying math or botany. This nonaccumulative learning *sees* the fact of conflict and ends it in the moment.

The words used in this book are direct and uncomplicated. There is no reason to use complex jargon. The words are not important; they are only descriptions used to communicate what one sees. The seeing, the actual observation, is the important thing. Too often, books on peace have been written about peace, using sophisticated verbiage that seems to create an understanding of the issue. But this is only a mental game, an exchange of lofty sounding ideas, that beguiles readers into thinking they know more about peace. Unfortunately, we fall in love with our words and, in so doing, create the illusion of understanding.

This book does not offer solutions, conclusions, or hopes about peace, and it does not present a particular method for achieving peace, nor is it an historical dissertation. It is meant only to initiate the process of enquiry, to begin to awaken, so to speak, insight into the core of conflict, not to expound voluminously on the seemingly endless theories and speculations that the overly educated brain has created in its search for "the answer" to the problem of war. Nor is this book offering any new philosophical, psychological, religious, or political approaches to solving the problems of war. All this book intends is to motivate the reader to look in a completely different way, to stimulate one's own enquiry into the causes of war — what prevents peace — so one can begin to question, to look anew at this tremendously urgent concern, and to begin to observe the nature and structure of conflict within oneself — that self which is all humankind. We have traditionally looked for the solution to war within a particular context or limited perspective. We have either approached war intellectually (abstractly) or emotionally, in reaction to its horrors. This has not brought about peace but has, rather, created further conflict. We have been looking in the wrong direction.

[Please note: By reading the three preceding books in this series, you will have a better opportunity to grasp the content of this book. The preceding books lay a foundation for understanding certain meanings of words used or observations presented, and will therefore give you a clearer view of what this book's intention is. However, you can read this book without the support of the previous books in the series if you have the focus and intensity to follow through, allowing the questions offered to act as a catalyst for finding out for yourself what it means to live without conflict, war.]

I
THE MORAL DILEMMA

TRADITIONAL APPROACHES
TO PEACE

As we begin to focus on the issue of peace, we need to look at how we have traditionally approached it. In what ways have we tried to bring about peace? Have these various approaches worked or have they, paradoxically, created more violence? It is important to look at how we have tried to bring about peace and understand war previously — to see how we might approach this differently now. If we don't, then we are left with what we already know, the timeworn theories and speculations on what will end war and create peace, those idealistic Utopian schemes that have only created confusion and more conflict.

Again, the intention of these observations is to raise fundamental questions about war and peace, to see how we have conventionally tried to solve this seemingly immeasurable problem, and to look from a radically* new perspective at what creates conflict, the substructure of war. For this to occur, we need only to begin the process. As we question, our sense of enquiry will take on a life of its own, and we can stop reading to observe directly — beyond the written word — what is actually happening.

*Radical means "at the root," to observe the cause or source of war and peace.

So, one must first observe what is — what we are actually doing now to create war and to bring about peace — without judgment, condemnation or justification. This is not an intellectual endeavor, but a real look at ourselves.

Where do we begin? How have we traditionally approached bringing about peace? What means have we used? What are we trying to accomplish in this book? Our main intention is to look at, observe, go into that which prevents peace, that which is not peaceful, and by a process of elimination of that which is not peaceful, we will come upon the positive — that is, peace, or freedom from conflict, war.

This book is offering a process to bring about peace. The conventional approach of creating the ideal of peace and emulating that ideal, as we shall see, only creates more conflict and, hence, war. The process of affirming peace through ideals is destructive! We will take another view, a radically different perspective, and challenge the traditional method of achieving peace by offering another approach — that of enquiry, the process of investigation by putting aside all that which is not peaceful. Understanding the difference between these two approaches is of paramount importance!

Now, where do we start with our investigation or enquiry into what is not peaceful? First, we need to look closely at the process we have conventionally used to bring about peace, to make sure that we are not merely advocating these same views in a different form in this book. One of our deeply held assumptions about how to create peace is that we must understand history, the past.

We have approached the understanding of war, the absence of peace, by examining history, the past, but has this aided us in ending war?

In schools, we teach history and we study past human interactions. The subject of history is marked by the succession of wars that mankind has produced throughout the centuries. Many historians assert that through the study of history, we can learn by our mistakes. If this were true, wouldn't we have understood how to end war hundreds of years ago? How many more wars will it take for us to find out how to end war?

Can we learn about war by acquiring knowledge about dates, names and historical perspectives? When we teach history to our children, what are we asking of them? We require memorization, the taking in of information to add to the knowledge they already have about the subject. Some people reason that if we accumulate enough information on the subject of war, at some point in the future we will understand how to end it. We have created libraries on the subject, and volumes on why we war and why there is no peace. We believe that the conventional process of learning, analyzing and synthesizing information, will create a solution. In science and technology, this type of thinking has a place, but we are attempting to understand human behavior and not a scientific or technological problem.

This book is not a political dissertation on peace. It is not advocating any political, economic or social "revolution." This does not mean that we should ignore the symptoms of war. We have created tremendous suffering and inequality in the world through hostile efforts to control and dominate others. This issue must be actively pursued and corrected. But we are ultimately concerned with ending conflict and bringing about lasting peace, not a temporary respite between conflicts. We are concerned with the understanding of war itself, not a particular war.

Can peace be brought about through a political movement? What is political reform? Is it the domination of one idea over others? Is it a way of thinking that screams, "This is the way. Ours is the ideal!" Doesn't this mean that other ideas are inherently in conflict with this "right" one? We have created socialism, communism, capitalism, totalitarianism, fascism, and other theories for the "good" of humankind. But each was based on separatism, resulting in the few controlling the many, or the few benefiting from the labors of others.

We are all human beings, but we don't see ourselves as being alike. Why is there a need to devise conflicting ways? We are so caught up in our differences that we perpetuate division into groups, with each reinforcing their own way. Why do we insist that we are different? And what does this have to do with war and the absence of peace?

There are many who will die for their differences, for their ideals, in the name of peace! They believe that war is peace and that conflict solves conflict.

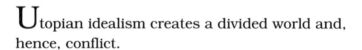

Utopian idealism creates a divided world and, hence, conflict.

Philosophy means "the love of truth" — not my intellectual idealism versus your idealism, stimulating the brain into pleasurable contemplation. In philosophical argument, we just go around and around in a maze of thinking.

Psychology presents various perspectives on the human condition. Freudians assert that we must analyze our past to see where the causes of conflict lie. Behaviorists say that we need to change our conditioning and set up new punishments and rewards to motivate us to live differently. The pioneers of Humanistic Psychology recommend peak experiences and self-actualization, which often results in self-indulgence. And there is a new movement in psychology called "Transpersonal" — consisting of rebellious outsiders to the mainstream world of clinical psychology who advocate various methods of self-transcendence, mainly supported by techniques from the Orient. Again, there are differing opinions, theories, conjectures and, hence, a lack of understanding of what universally creates and sustains conflict.

Can peace come about through conventional religious belief and practice? Established religious thinking, based on judgment and ideals, creates the struggle of good over evil. Traditional religious practice, regardless of sect or denomination, is founded on belief. Can belief solve the problem of war and bring about peace? Or does belief, whether it be religious, political, philosophical or psychological, create fragmentation — a world divided in thinking, a brain divided in itself? Belief is destructive for it is based on hope or faith, and is a postponement of acceptance of the actual. We hide behind belief, afraid to confront who we are because of the pain of the contrast between our actual behavior and that of the ideal.

We are not asking anyone to believe in what is written here. We are only encouraging each one's own questioning. Even though this book makes strong statements, these are meant only to stimulate questioning. If one can enquire for oneself into the truth of what is being said, then one's mind is active, alive, intelligent. If one engages in this process and discovers the falseness of what is said, the mind is also sharpening.

We are not asking anyone to join an "alternative" community dedicated to peace, or to rebel against society in any way. Rebellion is reaction and will never lead to understanding. Understanding is facing the fact directly, looking without prejudice — at society and ourselves.

We are not proposing "New Age" idealism, for there is no New Age! That is only an invention of our minds, an outcome of hopes based on fears. We are deluding ourselves if we imagine that we are any different than we have been for thousands of years. We remain tribal and primitive, violent, competitive and warlike. Technologically, we are advanced. Socially, we are undeveloped.

We are not advocating cynicism. We are interested in what is occurring in our lives each day. For a life as it really is — not as it should or should not be — is a reflection of truth.

We are saying over and over again that peace cannot come about through any idealistic means — which includes belief, hope, or faith in any form. Belief divides.

We are saying that there is a capacity that can understand conflict and eliminate war. However, to say that this process will bring about peace is dangerous, because we are so conditioned to be idealistic.

Again, it is important to remind ourselves that we are enquiring into the conditioned assumptions and timeworn beliefs we have about creating peace. We are not moving toward some conclusion, so that at the end of all this we will have "the answer," "the solution," "the Utopian plan." On the contrary, we will have no answer, no solution, no plan. All answers, solutions, plans are based on belief and, therefore, are divisive, and only create more conflict.

What we will have is nothing. Our conditioned thinking assumes that change produces something. But we are taking away, not building up.

Are we making sense? Or are we just advocating our own view, in competition with other views on the subject of peace? Are these observations fact or opinion? When is a statement an opinion or the author's philosophy, and when is it fact? Why are we so afraid of the facts of life? When we hold that there are only opinions about the causes of war, aren't we asserting that we know that there can only be opinions, that no one can understand what war is. This is a form of reverse arrogance, of asserting the negative: that there "cannot be." This "I don't know, so no one can know" belief becomes that person's truth and doesn't allow for the possibility that there can be an understanding and ending of war.

Can we consider, for a moment, that it might be possible for us to understand the cause of conflict, of war, and actually become free of it? Can our thinking be opened to the possibility that there may be a fundamental cause of conflict? Or have we become so convinced that we are "right" in the conclusion that no one can ever understand war, that we have given up enquiring?

Have we spent such a tremendous amount of energy in the political, religious, philosophical and psychological pursuit of peace that we have become cynical and apathetic? Or are we just too lazy or preoccupied to really question if there is a cause of war and the possibility of a lasting peace? Can we honestly look at these questions, or do we merely give intellectual lip service to them, entertaining these questions exclusively in the abstract?

Are we conditioned to believe that only an educated authority can answer these questions? Do we feel incapable of seriously considering that we may really be able to end war — not in the future through accumulating sophisticated knowledge — but now, through the direct perception of the roots of war within ourselves?

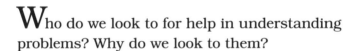

Who do we look to for help in understanding problems? Why do we look to them?

II
THE NEGATIVE APPROACH

WHAT PREVENTS PEACE

What is the process of finding out if questions/statements are true? Do we expect another to answer our questions for us? And where or who are they who can answer? What are we doing when we look to experts?

Can politicians bring about peace? Are they, by definition, divided in their views, this party against that party, in a power struggle over who is going to be on top? The politician is conditioned by his or her allegiance to a constituency of people, a nationalistic stance, and a particular brand of social justice — and, due to this divisive "loyalty," he or she is a perpetrator of conflict.

Can the general bring about peace? Isn't he or she dedicated to peace through war? However, the generals themselves wouldn't state it this way. They, like so many "experts," have created a special language (double-speak) that clouds the mind and creates the illusion of something else. In fact, the general is a warrior who believes that peace comes through the display or use of military might. When will we go beyond this illogical and destructive mentality? When does he or she stop being the general so there can be peace? If the logic is to create peace through strength, will peace come when each "side" is so powerful that one dare not attack the other, lest all are obliterated in war?

We are waiting for the "other," "them," to take the first step, to drop their defenses. But there is no other, no them! There is only us! So who will take the first step?

Can the priest, the religious leader, bring peace? One would think so since they profess to be dedicated to its pursuit. But in actuality, they too are divided in their ranks and levels of hierarchy, trying to establish who is the holiest within the particular religion or between different religious groups. At least military people are obvious in their expression of ironic, contradictory ideas! The religious pretend to be peaceful, following the ideals of their commandments, but they are at war within themselves, caught in the tangled judgments of good and bad. Each religion has its own brand of morality, each creating conflict. In essence, traditional religious practices reinforce the foundation of war through the conditioning nature of beliefs.

Can the doctor, the physician, bring about peace? Some people consider conflict a physiological disorder that can be cured with symptomatic remedies. Others believe that the problem is psychological and can be cured by analysis or mind altering drugs. Is this true, or are we again avoiding the central issue: that conflict is created by resistance to the fact of who we actually are? Resistance creates defensiveness, and psychological defensiveness creates social defensiveness. This social defensiveness manifests itself in competitive individualism, or in a collective group mentality. Either way, there is conflict inwardly and outwardly.

Can lawyers with their knowledge of arbitration bring about peace, or do they, by their confusing "legalese," distort the problems of relationship? Can the problems of relationship be solved through the courts, through expensive and emotionally exhausting legal means? We rely on lawyers and judges to bring criminals to justice, to deal with the symptomatic manifestations of conflict, but can they bring about an understanding of the causes of war?

We are concerned about the roots of conflict, of understanding war — not this war or that war, but war itself. Symptomatic approaches create surface solutions or reforms, which only sustain conflict and assuage the need for a deeper enquiry.

Can teachers, educators, help bring about peace? One would think that they could since the essence of education is relationship. Unfortunately, educators have traditionally concerned themselves with the accumulation of knowledge; knowledge has a place in living, but we are interested here in understanding behavior, relationship. The educator who is concerned with the whole child, interested in the child's psychological well-being, as well as his or her intellectual advancement, will want to understand the fundamental causes of conflict. The educator is the most important one in society — next, of course, to the parent — in caring for the child's needs. And yet the educator is not respected, professionally and economically. The educator has the best opportunity to find out what the cause of war is, but this means that he or she may have to leave the conventional educational system and perhaps even create a new school, for very few existing establishments are seriously interested in this issue of peace. As it is today, most educators are conditioning children to be warlike, to compete, to be aggressive, to get into the "best" universities and the most prestigious positions.

Can the newscaster, the person who reports our current events, bring about peace? These are important questions, because we so look to experts for understanding our lives. Television creates the expert in almost everything; all we have to do is turn them on and follow their recommendations. There are dozens of talk shows that give advice, from how to prevent tooth decay or invest in the stock market, to finding a compatible sexual partner. Experts are everywhere, and they especially abound on television. Newscasters or "anchor persons" are becoming the most celebrated of these television authorities. Anytime, 24 hours a day, they will inform us as to what is going on in the world. Some special "news shows" create forums for these reporters to "analyze" the events of the day, assuming that they have an understanding of the world situation. When confronted with an immediate, serious situation such as a brutal murder, most give worn-out sociological or psychological explanations, but must admit, when pressed, that the underlying causes remain a mystery.

We ask movie stars and super athletes what the cause of war is, or how to bring about peace, as if having their images projected on a 50-foot screen somehow qualifies them as experts on this subject.

We have even made criminals, murderers, war mongers, corrupt politicians and infamous "religious" leaders experts in understanding peace. Where is our dignity when we pay the criminal to tell us how to live?

Is the patriot an appropriate authority? Can the patriot, our paragon of national virtue, bring about peace? Or is he or she, by the very fact of his or her commitment to and identification with the fragmented nationalistic view, paradoxically the enemy of peace?

The patriot believes fervently in his or her country, above all else. He or she is the model of national pride, ideal defender of the faith and, by so being, is a powerful creator of conflict. Conflict is caused by the divisive state of mind that separates human beings into self-protective entities. My belief versus your belief, my country versus your country — each side identified with a particular cultural habit, each locked into a particular way of life. The patriot is the one who defends, to the death if need be, that separation, that state of antagonism — thus preventing a global perspective and unification of understanding.

Are authors who write eloquent books appropriate authorities because their views are published? Books on gardening or physics or travel are educational, and we can benefit from this type of authority being available to us. However, we are talking here about the psychological authority who advises us as to "how to live" and peddles his or her methods of success.

And then there are the "nonprofessional experts" and their plans and solutions for peace. Again, we are not trying to damage those people or organizations dedicated to peace. We are only questioning the process and method(s) used in the attempt to attain peace.

We have the "New Age Romantics," people who work to bring about world peace by "visualizing" it. They believe that in order to have a wonderful world, we have to imagine one. They visualize a world different from the one we have and see that we do not have to accept what exists now. But doesn't this "visualizing" create the ideal, the Utopia, the "should," and hence contribute to the conflict between what is and what ought to be?

Then there are the "We are One" proclaimers who assert that we are essentially all one, and that the only obstacle standing in the way of world peace is the inability to see the simple truths of our "real" nature. But this is also belief in an ideal, for the fact is that the human race is divided and fragmented. However, this doesn't mean that we should resign ourselves to this as inevitable and unalterable. Understanding the fact of that which divides us is the essence of intelligence and allows for freedom from division.

In the "peace" movement, we have "radical activists," well-meaning people advocating involvement in politics and the protesting of war, hunger, pollution, and all the social ills of mankind. We do need to constructively cope with our social problems at the level of reform, but unless we address the cause at the primary level, these problems will plague us forever.

The "violent revolutionaries" are also concerned with ending war and poverty, but they believe the way to achieve this is through violence. This is not an intelligent approach, obviously, but they are oppressed and frantic, and are reacting in desperation. All they know is violence, and they have seen how it has worked against them. They hope it can also work for them.

The "intellectuals" have pondered the problems of war for centuries. They read, and they write, and they lecture, and they receive awards and degrees. They have high ideals, educated solutions, lofty views; their words mystify and inspire. Do their words create peace, or do they cloud insight and confuse us?

Can organizations, such as those dedicated to peace, bring us freedom from conflict? An organization produces organized thinking, and is a vehicle for conducting business and carrying out administrative objectives. An organization is a practical, mechanical operation. Yet, many people become so identified with a particular organization, and so committed to its form and purpose, that the organization itself becomes the authority. Others give themselves over to an organization in their need for security in a world of chaos, and gain power and prestige through their association with the authority of a group.

Does looking at authorities in this way seem negative, cynical? Are we trying to tear them down with our critical observations, blaming them for our problems? Do we feel that they are responsible for our disorder, and that we are exempt? Is this what we are doing here?

Or are we looking at what prevents us from directly understanding our lives for ourselves? Can we, by a process of elimination, put aside all authorities who are unnecessary hindrances to self-discovery? Can we, through this process of elimination — or "negative" approach — come upon the truly positive? When we project an imagined positive, we create the authority and the need for emulation and worship of that authority. Can we look at our daily lives without the intervention of any psychological authority whatsoever? Can we become aware of how we act or react, observing our thinking, attitudes, beliefs, customs, traditions, all the habits that control our behavior? This is what can free us from conflict and the extremes of military war and the tyranny of authority. Being free, peace is there. Peace is not something to be sought; peace is a given, natural state of being. It is our conditioned way of thinking and behaving that prevents peace from occurring.

Are we using these observations as a mirror so we can see ourselves? We can either reject or accept what is being said, based on what we already know to be true, or we can use these observations as catalysts to look again at our assumptions. A simple, straightforward statement or question can awaken one's own perception to the truth or falseness of what is being offered. We are not trying to create more knowledge, accumulate more information on the subject of war and peace. As we read these words, what are our minds doing? Can we watch, as we read, to see how we are responding to these observations?

III
THE WAR WITHIN

CREATING THE ENEMY —
PEACE THROUGH
UNDERSTANDING CONFLICT

We have been looking at the various approaches to understanding peace and the conflict of war. We have also been examining the question of authority in relationship to the understanding of behavior. In essence, we have been exploring that which *prevents* peace, the viewpoints and the authorities that hold, assert and maintain a particular perspective. In order to have peace, we must put aside all that which prevents it: all the intellectual rhetoric and double-talk, and any authority with a self-protective, vested interest. This is a serious matter. One cannot be "emotional" or resentful, yet one must feel deeply, for without feeling these are merely words. Feelings connect us with the crucial actuality of our daily lives. Feeling deeply, one is motivated to act, not out of emotionalism, but out of insight into the nature of the problem. Insight has it own emotional effect, which is not the sentimentality of nationalism, patriotism, religious or political fervor.

Shall we look at peace and what prevents it at a deeper level? Can we look at the root, the fundamental cause of conflict? In order to bring about peace, we need to understand conflict. Trying to create peace is idealistic and therefore creates conflict. Shall we explore this together?

What does peace mean? Let's start with the commonly accepted meaning. According to Webster's Dictionary (which is an agreed upon, but not an absolute, authority), the meaning of peace is:

> "The absence of hostility, as in war; a state of harmony." Also, "Freedom from disquieting feelings and thoughts."

These two meanings are related. One looks outward at hostility, "as in war," and the other looks inward at "freedom from disquieting feelings and thoughts." Both the inner and outer are connected by the definition, "a state of harmony." Let's follow this a little further.

Peace also means "serenity," serenity meaning to be "still, silent" and "perfectly clear." Some synonyms for peace are: "order, union, reconciliation, unity."

Unity means "oneness, indivisibility, inseparability, integration, wholeness."

The title of this book states that peace is the "enemy of freedom." In other words, the conventional approaches to peace prevent freedom. We shall explore this, but first, let's examine what we mean by freedom. The commonly agreed meaning for freedom (according to Webster's Dictionary) is:

"A state of being free of constraints."

Constraint means to "keep confined, to restrain; arrest or use of force; compulsion; a restriction." A key word is compulsion, which means:

"An irresistible impulse to act irrationally."
Also, "coercive, obligatory."

We are looking at definitions, but we must be careful not to get caught in those descriptions. Words can be addictive, pleasurable. What we are trying to discover is another way to look at the problem, to find words that demonstrate the contradiction inherent in trying to bring about peace.

Peace is "wholeness, unity, harmony" — a state of mind that is "serene, still, silent" and "free from disquieting feelings and thoughts."

Can we bring about peace? What does this imply? How do we go about it? The "how" implies a method, a way to bring something about. And does trying to bring about peace prevent freedom — freedom being a state without "constraints," or "coercive, compulsory" behavior?

Let's look at an example that reflects the contradiction of trying to bring about peace — that is, a state of order and unity — through the process of compulsion, that which is coercive, obligatory. The United Nations is an international organization whose intent is to create world peace, order and cooperation. Is there an inherent irony in this approach? Has this organization succeeded in understanding and bringing about peace, or is it involved in a process that compounds the problem?

The word "united" means "one; whole." Can a unification of separate parts create a whole, as in the collection of nations coming together to create world order? Isn't there a contradiction in terms — united meaning "whole, indivisible, one," and nations meaning separate "groups of people organized as governments; tribes or federations"? Can we group "federations" into one undivided whole, while maintaining the isolated, fragmented tribal identification?

It seems simple enough to see that there cannot be wholeness when there is separation, that unity cannot come about when there is identification with the part. This defies logic and creates tremendous conflict. We think that by some magical means we can become one undivided human race, yet — at the same time — maintain our separation. This is a trick of the brain, an illusion. There can only be wholeness when there is wholeness. In other words, order, unity, one undivided world free of conflict — that is, peace — can only come about when each person sees that they are holding on to, and identifying with, the fragment.

Why do we do this? This identification creates conflict and prevents peace. In order to have peace, we must examine why we think we need to identify with the particular, the nationalistic fragment.

There are some who believe in wholeness and identify with a greater good than that of nationalism. But they end up with "my God versus your God," or a romantic tolerance that allows for all gods to be — in essence — one God, coexisting under the comprehensive ideal of wholeness. But again, there is separation caused by ideological thinking, no matter how expansive and universal the ideology seems to be.

What does identification have to do with peace preventing freedom? Can we look deeper into the structure of thinking that underlies this paradoxical statement?

How do we create peace? What are we doing to bring it about? We have looked at the outer, the political, economic, religious, philosophical approaches to peace, and none of these have brought peace. Now, can we look more closely, beneath the surface, to see what the method for trying to bring about peace is, inwardly?

We have touched upon identification as a factor that prevents peace. Let's examine this further. We seem to believe that through identification we can attain security and therefore be at peace. We identify with that which provides strength in numbers. We identify with the greater good. Be it through the group, the nation, the culture, the religion, or the god, the process is essentially the same: the creation of, and adherence to, the good or that which will keep us from the bad, the enemy of peace.

Where does this need for identification start? Does it begin in the classroom when we ask children to unquestioningly pledge their allegiance, to obey and defend their country against all foreign intruders? Or does it begin when we take children to a church, synagogue or mosque, and condition them to believe in a particular god or religious way of life?

Do we identify out of fear? What are we afraid of? Who are we afraid of? What is the enemy we fear? How does this fear come about? Can we go deeply into the structure of identification and its purpose, to see how it functions? Can we observe, like scientists, its operation within us?

Why do we need to identify, to "associate (oneself) closely with an individual or group?" To associate means to "join, to combine, unite." It also means "to connect in the mind," to "look in the imagination or mind." Identification or association is the process of the imagination (mind) that "links oneself with another or others." What effect does it have in the world when we identify ourselves with another or others, and form a separate unit?

Who do we associate or identify with? What are our ideals? Who do we want to be like? Who are our heroes? Are we identified with being an American, an Englishman, a Russian, a Jew, an Arab, or a Christian? Why? Do we think that this identification will give us security? And does it? Or does it sustain division and conflict? Is there security in a fragmented world? Does this create war? What is secure about that?

If we see the illogical and destructive outcome of identification, of associating with a particular ideology, why do we continue to do it? Is it a deep-seated habit, a firmly implanted conditioned response in our behavior?

How does identification, according to this type of illogical thinking, create peace? Let's examine the bare honesty of it, the core of the structure. Is it our need to be good, to live a virtuous and ethical life, that creates identification? Does desiring to be moral create conflict?

How do we become good? Let's suspend our examination of peace for a moment to look at this issue of goodness. What is goodness? We all want to be thought of as "good." We tell our children to be good — or else!

What is the process of attaining goodness? Some people believe that the child is "born in original sin," that he or she is, in essence, immoral ("bad") — and that what needs to happen is for the child to become "good."

So, in order to become good, one judges oneself and one's actions as bad and in need of redemption. Then the ideal of goodness (that which we should be, in reaction to that which we should not be) is created. We now have a dual state of mind and the battle of good over evil begins.

The brain has created an inner judge that describes what is bad and what is good, and whose task it is to eliminate the bad in favor of the good. This is where identification occurs. Identification, or association, involves emulation: living up to the ideal image of good, acceptable behavior, whatever that may be in one's particular culture. The brain is divided; on the one hand, it must suppress the bad and, on the other hand, it is obliged to be good. This process is the core foundation of conflict and is manifested in the world as global conflict. Look at this for yourself to see if it is true; observe yourself. One does not need to rely on an outside authority, for this involves direct self-observation — as it occurs. The challenge is to observe the nature and structure of thinking as it attempts to create good behavior.

The good represents what we should be or what we should do. One of the things we should do is be "peaceful," which is an ideal. The fact is that we are in conflict, divided within ourselves. Trying to be peaceful compounds the problem by intensifying the struggle between good and bad, which creates and sustains violent behavior.

Peace represents identification with the good: the national, political, religious or philosophical ideal. Identification is with others whose ideal is similar to our own because we have been indoctrinated, or conditioned, to do so through a system of punishments and rewards. Each society insists that its people identify with a particular brand of ideological thinking, the leaders of that society using their authority to maintain the status quo, and offering stability, security, order. Yet there is always a new ideal that emerges and generates change, either peacefully or violently.

Freedom means the absence of constraints: the ability to think for oneself, unhindered by fixed ideologies. Freedom isn't rebellion or the violent rejection of an old ideology in favor of a new one. Feeling coerced to be peaceful, or be good, is experiencing restriction: one is unfree when constrained by a particular way of thinking. Thinking itself involves the past, and must always be challenged in the movement of life. When we are forced to act as we should, to be good or peaceful, then that compulsion can lead to an "irresistible impulse to act irrationally." Formulating rigid beliefs, systems to live by, does not lead to rational acts. Acting rationally involves the ability to think clearly, logically, sanely — thinking that emanates from observation itself. Living according to the conditioned dictates of a particular society is not sane.

There is also the question of what happens to the bad or that which is not ideal. What does the brain do regarding that which does not fit in with its ideal? It assigns power to something outside itself. In this way the "Devil" is created, an evil entity that causes the problem inside us. "It is the 'Devil' who's doing this! I need to drive him out and bring 'God' back into my life." This attributing of a quality of our own behavior as coming from an outside source (whether bad or good) denies responsibility for our own actions. We hold the view that IT (Devil or God) will either destroy or save us. We cannot see that we are creating this struggle of good over evil, and the conflict this produces. In the sociological or political context, we assign the bad to "them": the enemies, the terrorists — and the good to "us": the heroes, the freedom fighters.

But the war within, whether it manifests in religious, political, or sociological terms, is essentially the same: a struggle of the brain in a quest to be "good."

Identification creates sides and heroes, with idealistic images of what a hero should be varying according to the culture. But the hero is usually the patriot, the one who carries the banner of goodness against all enemies, "foreign and domestic." All sides see themselves as heroes and freedom fighters. And God, of course, is on the side of good — but each side sees itself as good. Don't we see this paradox?

Each "side" depicts the enemy as greedy, murderous, villainous, and out to rape, pillage and plunder. Each side sees itself as the "victim," defending itself against the "mad dog" enemy. Each side feels justified, in the name of their God and Holy Book, in protecting themselves and slaying the villain — for righteousness' sake.

But this vision of the "enemy" is nothing more than the projected judgment of ourselves, the condemned image of how bad we think we are. What prevents us from coming into direct contact with this judgment, this self-condemnation, this "evil" person that we think we are, is the fear of how others will regard us. We have created a self-consciousness about our "bad" side, a conscience that guides us. The judgment of our behavior as bad is more than image or thought, it is also feeling. Feeling bad is painful, so it is no wonder that we don't want to look at ourselves directly.

How is this process sustained? In the same way that we control the behavior of our pets: we subject ourselves to a system of rewards and punishments through conditioning. The ultimate reward is Heaven or the punishment Hell, if one is of that religious persuasion. Or the process manifests in social castigation and disapproval from our peers. The rewards bestowed by society are degrees, testimonials, wealth, status. There are multifarious punishments and rewards. The particulars aren't as important as understanding the basic need for, and process of, controlling behavior — which comes from needing approval and wanting to be liked as the projected self-image of the good person we think we should be.

It is easy to see the political or religious manifestations of idealization. The Arabs and the Israelis, the Russians and the Americans, the Iraqis and the Iranians, all divided into opposing ideological camps that are fundamentally rooted in the structure of trying to live according to a formulated Utopian system. Idealized projections are, essentially, the brain's attempt to bring about good behavior. We are not aware that the problem lies within us, and we approach the solving of war with the same technique that generates it — the creation of ideals.

So, the war within is created by the brain trying to produce goodness and virtuous living through ideals; it is thinking that is the cause of the problem. Thinking as a tool of measurement, comparison and evaluation functions in the realm of science and technology as it should, but when this same form of thinking is applied unquestioningly to the psychological realm in trying to change behavior, there is perpetual conflict and violence. So, we are challenging the use of a comparative tool to change who we are psychologically. In the psychological area, as in the scientific, thinking does what it always does: it judges, compares, evaluates — thereby creating good and bad.

Fundamentally, at the root of conflict, is this destructive process of conditioned thinking that moralistically judges behavior in favor of some idealized image of correct and virtuous action. Trying to be nonviolent, to be "good," as we have discussed, paradoxically creates conflict and violent behavior. So our endeavors to be peaceful or nonviolent create the opposite effect.

When peace or nonviolence becomes the ideal, judgment follows and conflict ensues. This is fundamental.

We look at the symptomatic issues and attempt to solve our problems through reform. Rarely do we go beneath the surface to look at the root of the problem within ourselves.

We are investigating conflict that is created by ideological thinking concerned with bringing about order, harmony, unity — that is, peace. Are we beginning to see the paradox: that the conventional process of bringing about peace is conflict producing?

We started out by examining the traditional approaches to peace, the conventional ways to free ourselves of conflict. And we moved from there to examine how that process, through the emulation of, and adherence to, psychological authority only sustains conflict, inwardly and outwardly. We have been looking at all this anew, observing — at the same time — the brain's reaction as we read these pages. So we are learning as we go, not collecting information or knowledge on the subject of war and peace, but actually awakening observation into the brain's workings, its nature and structure, as thought occurs each moment. This awakening of observation is the faculty of intelligence, not IQ, that has an inherent capacity to "know" what is true, right. It is this intelligence that will understand conflict and bring about peace — not through ideals, but actually — in the moment. And this intelligence will have an effect on our relationships with others, and on the concern of humankind worldwide for global order and well-being.

Have we arrived at an understanding of what this book and these observations are intending? Do we need to read on concerning what creates conflict, how we bring about violence in our quest for a nonviolent way of living, how we kill the spirit of enquiry through our need for authorities in the area of relationship? As we said at the start, one can, at any time, stop reading and go beyond the printed word to observe the actuality of conditioned thinking as it occurs in us, for it is conditioned thinking, the process of changing behavior through ideals, that is at the root of conflict. But how will we know if this is true, or not? Who is there to tell us? Do we need to try all the conventional avenues before we can be aware of their dead ends? What is the correct thing to do? Or is this the wrong question?

If we have been following all this and have been actively questioning, creatively doubting, what the conventional, conditional views are and, at the same time, questioning what is being presented in this book, what is our state of mind now? Have we been able to put aside all that which is not peaceful? Has this "process of elimination" helped free our minds from the conventions of traditional, antiquated thinking? When one has clearly, step by step, enquired into that which is disorder, chaos and confusion — that thinking which creates conflict, war — can there be peace of mind? Have we understood the significance of this process: that peace comes about when we put aside, through careful investigation, all that which creates conflict? Have we understood that the pursuit of peace — the creation, affirmation, and emulation of idealistic, "peaceful" behavior — paradoxically creates conflict, disorder and, at the extreme, war? Have we seen to the depths of this, to the root within the make-up of how we think? If we don't understand the cause, we cannot end the problem! However, if we are involved in this process, then peace, real freedom from conflict, is occurring — now! — as we are enquiring intelligently into life.

VIII
WHERE DO WE GO
FROM HERE?

It seems that if one is observant and has questioned the underlying structure of what prevents peace and creates conflict, then there is a realization that reading about peace is not necessary! This book, or any book for that matter, can only reflect what is either true or false. It is ultimately up to the reader to see for him or herself the truth or falseness of the content. In this case, words written on a page are only pointers, metaphors, symbols for what the author is asking the reader to look at. Many times, books on war and peace are merely exciting (or boring) descriptions of symptomatic manifestations of historical perspectives; or fanciful projections based on the vivid imagination of the author; or highly obtuse, sophisticated, intellectually clever interpretations of the overly educated brain. Rarely do we look simply at the obvious reality of our everyday life and see that *we*, our conditioned attitudes, prevent peace!

We are a collection of highly conditioned individuals seeking security in our own self-projected beliefs. We have been conditioned from birth to believe in our parents, teachers, religious and political leaders, in our country, flag, and our particular idiosyncratic worship of what we consider God.

This conditioning is who we are. It is an eclectic accumulation of information that forms our thoughts and behavior. Being conditioned, we are isolated in that conditioning; we are fragmented by solitary, self-serving beliefs. These belief systems make up our consciousness, and through that consciousness — that accumulation of conditioning — we act. And, in so doing, we create conflict in the world.

When one becomes aware of that state and sees the futility of acting out of fragmentation and isolating, conditioned belief systems, what usually happens is that one reacts or rebels and, in so doing, more conflict is created. Or one finds another belief system to free oneself from the tyranny of a former way of life. Neither rebellion nor alternative belief systems can end conflict! Both, in fact, sustain it!

Reading through this book, one comes to the realization that the very process of enquiry, of really looking at the questions we are asking, creates a highly sensitive, alert, intelligent state of mind, a mind that is observant, cautious. It is this alertness, this cautiousness, that recognizes one's own conditioned responses to life and, in so doing, ends them as they arise. At first this may require hindsight, becoming aware of how one has been in the past. But as one continues to explore, to enquire, time diminishes in importance and one can see the conditioned response as it is happening. If one stays alert, then that creative cautiousness makes it possible for the continuous dissipation of the tendency and compulsion for habitual, conditioned thinking.

Have we understood all of this? Have we seen the futility and destructiveness of identification, of belief systems? Have we understood the paradoxical nature of trying to bring about peace through idealistic thinking? Have we observed the creative potential for understanding what prevents peace by negating that which is not peaceful and creates conflict? And, have we felt the tremendous importance of what this can mean in our relationships worldwide? Or are we still convinced that we are right, that conventional approaches to ending war and bringing about peace are viable solutions? Which is it?

For thousands of years we have tried to end war and live peacefully — and for thousands of years this goal has not been reached. When will we end war — not a particular war, but war itself? It is not enough to temporarily contain conflict in some particular symptomatic instance. War is our way of life; it is everywhere. To feel that we now will have peace in the U.S.A. because the U.S.S.R. is beginning to change indicates a limited, self-centered view. Conflict is a global human issue and pervades all of life — from the home to the school and political or religious institutions. Unless we get to the root of conflict, it will remain with us forever. Does this make sense?

Where do we go from here? We start to question, to probe, to investigate the myriad of conditioned assumptions and prejudices about living. We create schools that put this vital challenge at the forefront of their curriculums. We help our children in not accepting war as a solution for creating peace. We help them to see the possibility of ending war, not for a limited time, but to end it permanently. Unless we keep ourselves open to this possibility, we will, by our resignation to the inevitability of war, keep conflict alive for our children, to be passed down century after century as it has been in the past. It is up to each one of us to look at ourselves, to understand how we *prevent* peace and therefore create conflict. And in so doing, conflict ends and peace is there — naturally, without effort, because there is intelligence.

Portrait: Earl Bates

Terrence Webster-Doyle, Ph.D. was Founder and Director of three independent schools and has taught at the secondary, community college and university levels in Education, Psychology and Philosophy. He has worked in Juvenile Delinquency Prevention and has developed counseling programs for teenagers. He has earned a Doctorate Degree in Psychology, a 5th degree black belt in Karate, and has studied and taught the Martial Arts for over 30 years. He has also produced numerous conferences and workshops on New Directions in Education. Currently, he is Director of the Shuhari Institute, a Center for the Study of the Martial Arts, Director of the Atrium Society, and Co-director of the Atrium School whose intent is to explore psychological conditioning.

ABOUT THE PUBLISHER

Atrium Society concerns itself with fundamental issues which prevent understanding and cooperation in human affairs. Starting with the fact that our minds are conditioned by our origin of birth, education, and experiences, Atrium Society's intent is to bring this issue of conditioning to the forefront of our awareness. Observation of the fact of conditioning, becoming directly aware of the movement of thought and action, brings us face-to-face with the actuality of ourselves. Seeing who we actually are, not merely what we think we are, reveals the potential for a transformation of our ways of being and relating.

If you would like more information, please write or call us. We enjoy hearing from people who read our books and appreciate your comments.

Published by:
Atrium Society
Post Office Box 816
Middlebury, Vermont 05753
Tel: (802) 388-0922
Fax: (802) 388-1027
For book order information:
(800) 848-6021

Other books written by
Terrence Webster-Doyle

<u>FOR ADULTS</u>
• **Growing Up Sane**:
Understanding the Conditioned Mind
• **Brave New Child**:
Education for the 21st Century
• **The Religious Impulse**:
A Quest for Innocence
• **Karate**:
The Art of Empty Self*
• **One Encounter, One Chance**:
The Essence of Take Nami Do Karate**

<u>FOR YOUNG PEOPLE</u>
• **Facing the Double-Edged Sword**:
The Art of Karate for Young People***
• **Tug of War**:
Peace Through Understanding Conflict
• **Fighting the Invisible Enemy**:
Solving Conflict Peacefully
• **Why is Everybody Always Picking on Me?**:
A Guide to Handling Bullies

*Winner: Benjamin Franklin Award — New Age/Metaphysical
**Finalist: Benjamin Franklin Award — Psychology/Self-Help
***Finalist: Benjamin Franklin Award — Interior Design, and
Winner: Award of Excellence, Ventura Ad Society